Aporia.

Camila van Wuijckhuijse

BookLeaf Publishing

India | USA | UK

Presentation by *BookLeaf Publishing*

Web: www.bookleafpub.com

E-mail: info@bookleafpub.com

ISBN: 978-93-5744-966-3

First edition 2022

DEDICATION

Voor Melis.

snap

if i were to love you
any more than this,
my heart would snap
right into two
and i'd chase the sky
even more so than now

-

an acrobatic dance
with the devil

-

if i were to love you
any harder than this,
my heart would outstretch
the kissing horizon
and i'd drown into the sky
right into nothing

Bright Butterfly

But if (not when) someone leaves
A bright butterfly in my throat,
How do I breathe;
How do I speak?
But when, not if, my lips ache
Of honey-drunk kisses,
I fall, fall -
Fast asleep.

-

Caught within a blanket of blush;
Cradled by your absence, I fall,
Fall;
Fast asleep;
While a bright butterfly sings
Of a spring sweeter than honey;
In my dreams,
Falling.

Faint

The dizzy comes, it rushes in
to my head, like a spell;
I feel the faint, it lifts me up
to a different kind of self.

My body rushes, sits me down
to a breath, for me to take;
I feel some life, remember my Self -
oh, to feel alive,

I take.

The skinned wolf

I put a plaster on a crust
That remained on a wound
Somewhere, in the forest
Of my mind

You complain:
It won't heal fast
Enough, you say,
As you rip off the only help

I ever offered myself;
Not me but your fury
Strips me bare,
Leaving me alone

To bleed
From a wound which has lost
Its crusty shield -
Exposed,

For everyone to mock and marvel,
Like an emaciated, skinned wolf
On a pile of flowers.

I tied my hair

I tie my hair, with skinny strings,
to the stars, so when the wind sings,
over seas afar, they electrocute my hair,
into the dancing web of a spider,
making it move to the magical melody
of many millions of little lights
that couldn't shine any brighter.

I tied my hair to thin branches
of towering trees, so when the wolf howls
at the mighty moon she sees, and my hair's
flying
'round my ears in some seasonal breeze,
it'll pull the strings to my heart's precious things,
so I can still so clearly hear
the song the lone leaf sings.

A Distant Comfort

I'm slipping away;
through my very own fingers, I slip.
Is it maybe true after all,
do some people just not know
how to cope with themselves?

We simply carry too much around;
too much fear that seeks out
comfort; don't we all get cheated on -
in one way or another -
by life, at one point

or another; when the sky starts to fall,
and you are the only one there
to catch it; you have no choice
but to choose -
do you look up or down?

In this, the sky alone can't comfort me;
a very fearful breath to take,
indeed; when you feel as distant
as the moon, I can feel myself,
slipping away

again;

through my very own fingers
I slip, because you are not the moon
to me; you are the entire sky.
You chewed up the moon and left

a darkness in which I cannot
tell the up from the down;
and in this, you alone
can't comfort me. When you swoop
and start your fall, I slip;

away, I feel myself slip
through my very own fingers.
Swallow me whole
(if I can't catch you) -
let me sleep on the moon tonight.

softly

sleepless nights and a heart filled with love;
i numb my tastebuds with cigarettes and
tasteless dreams;
life kills, sleeping is tiresome;
the heart wants what the heart wants.

when the thoughts are ugly
and there is no room for the pretty;
sometimes it's better not to think

out
loud.

Cloud 9 (pt 1)

Did you ever hear the butterflies sigh?
Did you see them try
to catch their breath mid-flight, and fight
till hell started freezing over?

Did you fear the flutter of their wings?
Did you taste their stutter
on the tip of your tongue, and sing
if Love is a circle, we go round, too?

Cloud 9 (pt 2)

Did you ever throw away a wish?
Did you forget to kiss
when you wished Love well, and lose her
to a frozen wishing well?

The balancing act of the butterfly;
its flutters stuttering smoke signals through
Cloud 9;
if Love is a circle, you are, too;
When she goes gone and, well, denies you

your tears to cry
are not your own.

Somewhere

Somewhere between
the kiss from your lips
and the skies of Lisbon

flies my breath

amidst
wings of butterflies
I catch, I bite
a bit

(Joy)
from the past

Breath

Death is -
and it's in the daily;
The getting up
then falling
and then the getting up
again

Death is -
The breathing, the flying;
the suspense, the kissing (or the hanging);
between the inhale and the exhale, oh -
the breathing. There is death
in the breath.

Sometimes

Sometimes;
I sing sweet lullabies in my sleep;
Or stalk around like a zombie;
Lost for words, looking to find a way;
Dancing my way -
back to you

Sometimes;
This is where the story goes on;
We've called it a day;
and I'm humming the night
a way away -
always back to you

Swinging

When your hands settle
upon my soul,
I find myself all over
again, swinging
from the stars,
dancing on the wind.

11th Hour

It is the eleventh hour –
The world is flat again, and
Babies in bars fall asleep,
Milk bottle still in hand.
They simmer into sweet slumber,
And see before their black eyelids
The depth of the White
Russian's gun barrel.
So early it is for such
Carefully constructed corruption;
For when the babies wake, and
It is not yet the spring time,
They will think the shit
In their diapers normal –
They will not even smell it, –
Just as when they hang
From the sharp edge of this world,
They will not feel
Their fingers
bleeding.

Sharing is caring

When we were told
How sharing is caring;
And, haven't you heard
Of the cry of the siren;

A loving desperation,
A hopeful exasperation;
Once given it is lost,
A thousand times over.

I was a fairy

When I was small, I was a fairy;
Then I grew up, into a power ranger.
When she was small, she was unavailable;
Then she grew up, or maybe she didn't.

He sees a calm creek;
I fear an avalanche.
We hide behind who we are;
It's what keeps us as we are.

—

Where does solace lie;
Does it hide within our Selves?
She finds it safe, a lingering pain;
I feed tragedy with normalcy.

I feed it mist and dewdrops;
Others feed the little fairy.
Walking somewhere on the clouds I sing;
I am yeah, and it is all I want to know.

—

We sense who someone is;
But whence did the cracks come from?

Past is dead, future in labour;
A moment is born, a collision of both.

Every time we hear those songs;
How we crawl into the notes.
So when thunder strikes again, we'll sing;
We'll share a touch of sensitricity.

—

When I was small, I was a fairy;
Theatrical music buzzed in my ears.
When he was small, he would go digging;
He would paint portraits of his mysteries.

Let us pretend we know it all;
Let us be grown-ups now.
Let's cut off our wings and mourn;
Put down the brush, visit a museum.

Sorry

Shower me
In butterfly kisses and regret,

So I can believe you
When you say to me, 'Sorry -

That was the worst thing
I have ever said,'
And love you endlessly again.

In Orbit

I carry the night sky
in my stomach,
cradle the fallen stars
and planetary mysteries,
while still untangling
the knots we merged
in orbit.

www.ingramcontent.com/pod-product-compliance
Lightning Source LLC
Chambersburg PA
CBHW070736160726
48003CB00006BA/2533